AWAKEND

_hydrus

Published by: Hydrus
Graphics by: Hydrus
Proofreading by: Gabrielle G.
Cover Design by: Cleo Moran - Devoted Pages Designs
Formatting by: Cleo Moran - Devoted Pages Designs
https://www.devotedpages.com

Manufactured in the United States of America

ISBN: 978-1-7357824-0-9

Impressions of the love
that you etched in my soul
will always live in the ink I bleed
and the tears I weep

_hydrus

Dedicated to everyone we have lost

Tarots cards, much like poems, have the ability to paint a vivid picture of what once was or what could be.

They delve into the subtleties that we all carry within ourselves and the secrets that make us who we are.

Awakend is an immersion into the world of tarot and its mysteries.

Read it one way, then another, and let the words guide you into the meaning of each card. Allow chance and curiosity to
accompany you on this incredible journey and let your heart awaken to hope even
after having thought everything was lost.

And who knows what secrets you might find out about yourself...

You awakened my soul
with the only darkness I ever loved

_hydrus

Your beautiful darkness is as
endless as the light buried in your heart

_hydrus

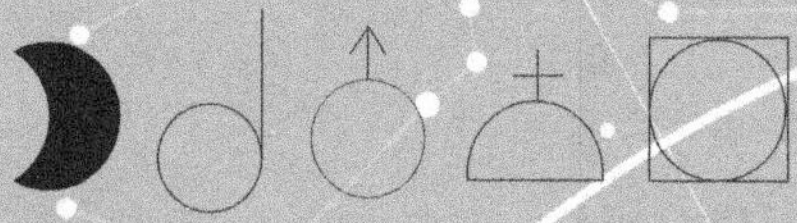

Upright: unconscious, illusions, intuition

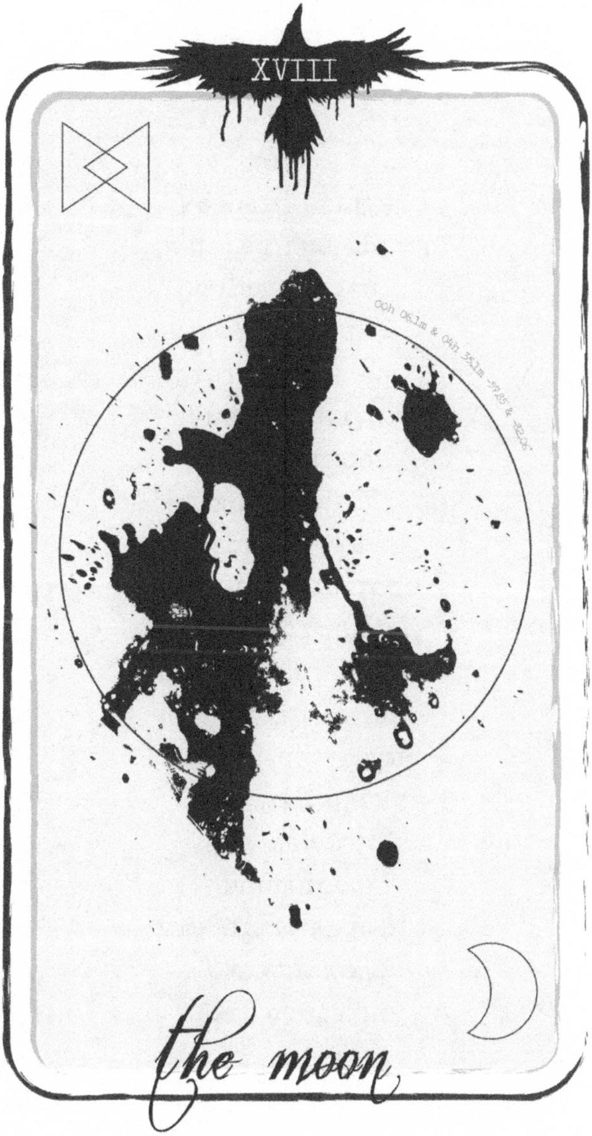
XVIII
00h 06.1m & 04h 35.1m -59.85 & -82.06
the moon

A box contains
My every move
Categorized simple
Understood
One way in
One way out
Detained within
Cluttered doubt
Distracted actions
Entangled shame
Familiar tensions
Helpless lanes
Lost meaning
Purpose fades
Another wall
Behind a shade
A keyless entry
Captive life
Ensnared the spirit
Keepers strife

Suspect
_hydrus

I chased a storm
To feel its wrath
Take its form
Wreak its path
Once inside
I met the sun
A thunderous guide
We became one
The moon and stars
In a jealous rage
Casted wind
To disrupt our fate
Rains would cease
The clouds would dry
Forgotten peace
My empty sky

Luna
_hydrus

Empty the notes that I write
Silent the pain still in sight
Abandoned the ink that I spill
Removed from my life that was killed

No return
_hydrus

In my dreams you will feast
Living off my silent needs
Whispered hymns you recant
Hypnotic sweet circumstance

Maidens dance to appease
In my trance one will please
Quiet slumber beckons screams
It was not what it seemed

Incubus
_hydrus

Moonlit shadows thrown on walls
Brackish cats scream eerie calls
Nameless corners obscure your way
Unfamiliar secrets stalk their prey

Followed footsteps slight and near
Dreadful patience drowned in fear
Aroused intentions sensed to strike
Paralyzed trembles allured to fight

Stalked in silence stricken to flee
Restrained despair in stone effigy
Amongst the specter panic now looms
Caught by the shadow impending the doom

Lost in the struggle all fears go black
Phobic duress in an anxious attack
Deadly the outcome a body lays soaked
All due to the actions you provoked

Vigilant
_hydrus

Slumped in your pain you fell
A questionable instinct or spell
Your vision of worth collapsed
Perception has dwindled at last

Untold miseries repeat
Hunched over accepting defeat
Longing for closure persists
Unwanted exposure exists

One must dwell in a state
Confusion entices debates
Untold illusions will creep
Voices will mimic in sleep

An alter has risen inside
Here the hosts will reside
Reality blurred by the strain
Emotions have silenced the sane

Suffering
_hydrus

An unknown shadow quietly waits
Expecting a sandmans taste
Obsessively bedding my side
Amongst me believed to have died

Lost in the scars I have seen
Continues to haunt and scheme
Frozen my actions lay still
Cold to the touch is his thrill

Darkness has drained all the light
Frightened in life I survive
Desperately lurking instead
Alone in bed I am dead

Company
_hydrus

Suspicious the moment we met
In your tears was witnessed regret
Ironic this meeting would be
Eroded was my sympathy

The sudden appearance of sin
Presented with a tainted grin
Allured me to only surmise
A moment that hinted demise

Quick to the vision at hand
My soul must cling to the plan
Trust had taken new form
Eyes were betrayed and forewarned

The end my heart will declare
Impressionable signs are impaired
Although one may not comprehend
Your actions destined your end

Suddenly
_hydrus

I am lost in what we could be
Our lives drowned in ecstasy
Confusion drawn all from fire
Falsehoods just built on desire

Misread
_hydrus

How dare you retreat into my dreams
Secluded from all and what may seem
Playing a game you cannot win
Eclipsed in twists and spiraled spins

Subconsciously I ask for a wish
An enlightened request you permit
Let my slumber at peace be my state
Defeated until I awake

Selfish
_hydrus

Hollowed moans stare in sleep
As the hands begin to creep
Awaiting a stolen glance
Is the stare of an eerie trance

The dead reside in my room
Inflicting the noises of doom
If only the shadows would flee
And let the dark slumber just be

Bedtime
_hydrus

All of a sudden
Chills catch my breathe
A moment of sadness
Evoked in distress

Awakened inside me
Voices scream
Nervous the logic
Unknown the extremes

Wishfully happened
One must explore
Madness abandoned
Limitless doors

Have I just imagined
A sense quite irate
Leaving resemblance
Of a horrible fate

Sensed
_hydrus

Why must you
Tease my lips

I yearn for
A simple sip

Mention of us
Escapes

Confusion
Is all I taste

Uncomitted
_hydrus

Water ripples
Waves dance on glass
Empty space
A distant glance

An open window
A slight breeze escapes
Tapping a finger
Mental the wait

Quietly listening
Time just sits
Awaiting disturbance
Tingling persists

Along with an echo
Suggestions lay claim
Trusting the guidance
I am given a name

Beyond
_hydrus

Distant murder
Faintly voiced
Swarming hexes
Perched and poised
Gleaming feathers
Dipped in blood
Sharpened talons
Misunderstood
Keeping watch
Their hosts await
Calculating
Watchful fate
Wings surround
A shadowed face
Hoisted anvil
Set to slay
Upon a stone
That grass evades
Tattered ropes
Cling to slate
Jekylls smirk
Plague the flight
Darkened moon
Receives the night

Raven
_hydrus

Hazy the moment
A veil brushed aside
Clever the servant
Inside me resides

Rendered his whispers
Continued the urge
Condemned by habits
Obsessed with the purge

Affecting my conscious
Discovered ordeal
Repressed existence
Numb in the feel

Persistent voices
Abusive in all
Destructive knowledge
I rise as I fall

Motionless
_hydrus

Who resides in my room
Harps my soul full of gloom
Never weds keeps me near
Pulls me close hosts my fear
In the end I regret
Simply there as her pet

Serpent
_hydrus

Delusions await
As the fingers exclaim
Enchanted the words
Methodic the games

Performed in deception
Vanished the hope
Relentless the tricks
As the mind tries to cope

Vast are the myths
Uncovered to awe
Spellbound by smiths
Conceived to the fall

Regardless the outcome
A path has been placed
Left with the burden
Perceptions erased

Doubt
_hydrus

Waves of color transcend all light
Thoughts misguided with stolen sight

Recovered senses of a distant time
When we awoke so intertwined

Many winters and the newest blooms
Empty walls and secluded rooms

In the dark my visions still can see
Crescent moons that illuminate me

Dusk filled skies of a life not lived
Mistaken love with none to give

Eclipsed horizons under dying stars
Far removed from my eternal scars

Lens
_hydrus

I have a feeling
Things will burn
A constant advisor
Who will not learn

Choices abandoned
Left to scorch
Wielded emotions
Entitled to torch

Listening to conjures
Exclaiming repent
Content in their magic
Retained in descent

Obstructed the witness
Flames still obey
Crafted to question
Impressions will pay

Optical
_hydrus

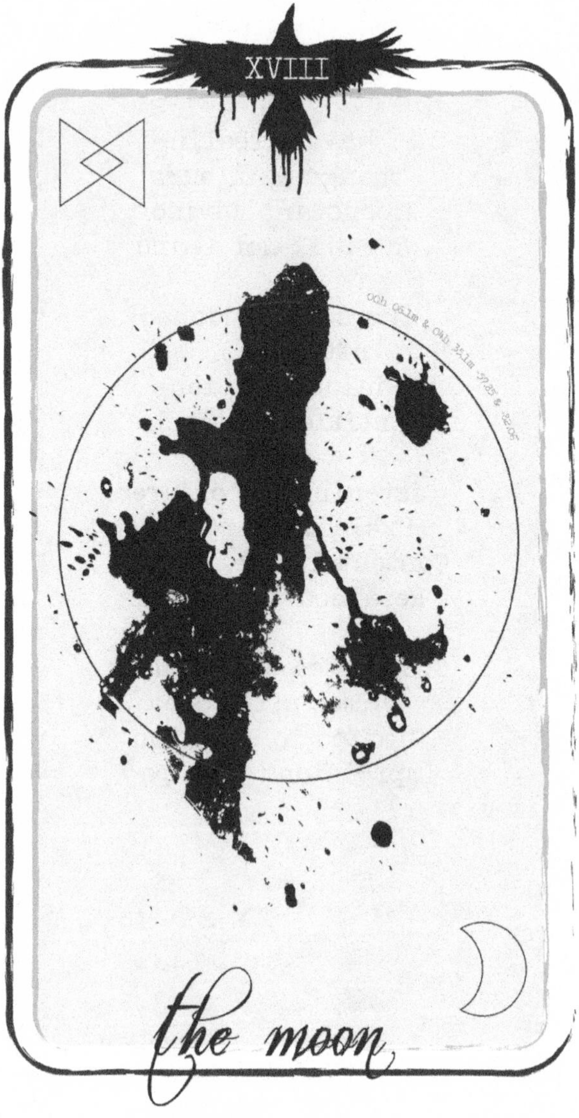
XVIII
00h 05.1m & 04h 35.1m -57.25 & -82.05
the moon

Reversed: confusion, fear, misinterpretation

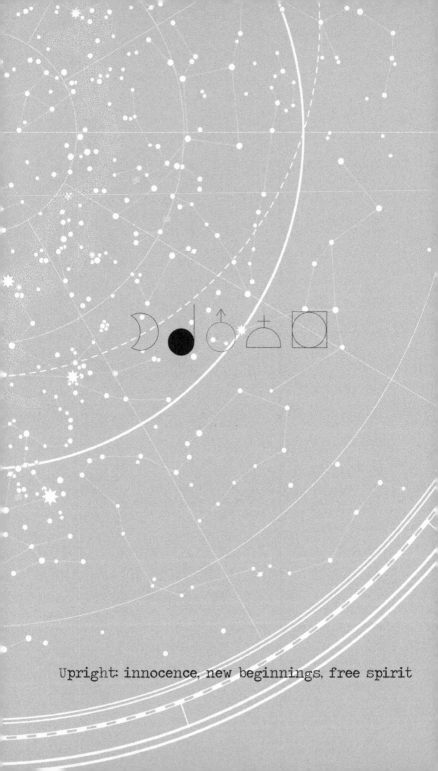

Upright: innocence, new beginnings, free spirit

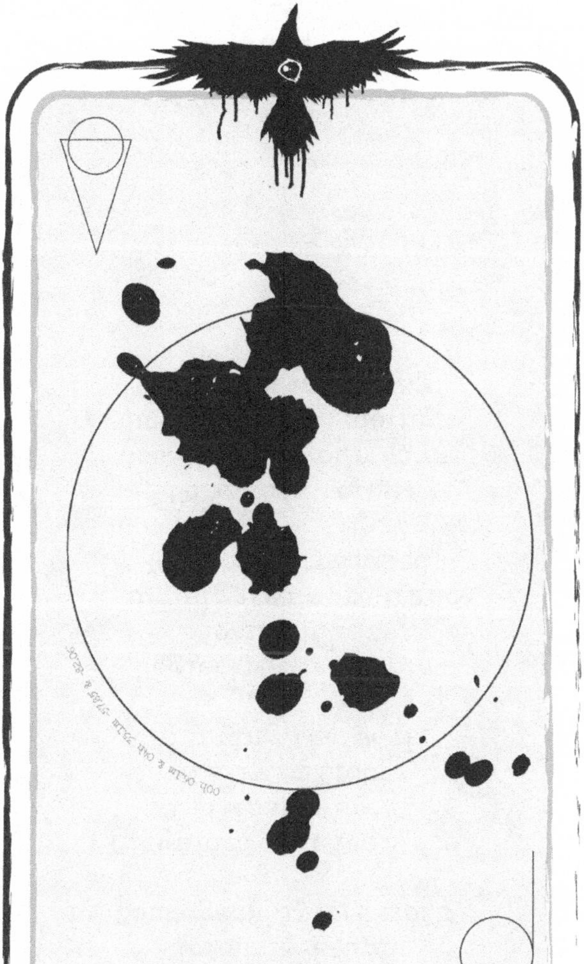
the fool

Who gave you the right
To be so senseless
Viciously stupid
Courageously reckless

Misguided and fearless
Mindless to speak
Wildly callous
Taunting the weak

Neglectfully simple
Idiotic in gaze
Short-sighted appearance
Ruthlessly phrased

Merciless being
Obsolete in your ways
Unwise in your doings
Alone you will stay

Fossil
_hydrus

An honest composure
Naive to the sense
Developed from atom
Convicted penance

Instructed in life
Righteously told
Expand new horizons
Learn from the old

Vast was the vision
Curiously vain
Naked the reflections
Broken the chain

Hunger too great
Questions arose
Judgement in haste
Sentence imposed

All that was known
Must be retried
No more the idol
Live now to die

Innocence
_hydrus

A heartless word
Sudden laughs
Spoken jest
Misplaced gaffes

Pointy letters
Arranged to spite
Quick attacks
Always right

Questioned path
Internal thoughts
Trapped reactions
Lessons taught

Uncaring stooge
Impulsive ape
Obnoxious brute
I must escape

Thoughtless
_hydrus

Guided by winds
Broken in form
Flowing in strength
Colliding by storms

Depths of the oceans
Touching the stars
Eclipsed in horizons
Arisen from far

Invisibly agile
Its reach has no bounds
Intimately fragile
Infinitely sound

Eternal the message
A beauty within
Courageously humble
Free of its skin

Spirit
_hydrus

Night has passed
We lay away
Contemplating
Things to say
Morning comes
Feelings flow
An attachment
Need to know
All that angst
Hear ones tone
Only spent
Over the phone
Shortly there
Time forgets
Words become
Morning regrets
Quick to say
Unkindly things
Callous actions
Remarks will bring
Moody blurbs
Day begins
Uncaring norm
Reality wins

Undue
_hydrus

A chapter has started
Unknown is the draft
Willing the reader
Intended the path

End is unclear
Sands in a glass
Deviated the pace
Thrown to the vast

Amending your fortune
As the pages run bare
Restarting a sentence
Actions unclear

Retracing your steps
Mapping the time
Discouraged regrets
Eternal the climb

Challenges still steep
Devised to impede
Long in this journey
Must fail to then lead

Onward
_hydrus

Your words
Pounced like lions
A strength
I obtained
Incredible hunger
For a loss
Once attained
In sadness and weakness
Your hands held me high
A bond and a moment
That started the lie
That was the instance
I opened my heart
Slow and persistent
You tore it apart
Ripped for accepting
Unharnessed abuse
Resenting the moment
You tightened your noose

Captured
_hydrus

An unbound whisper
Birthed to just be
Divine independence
Unimpeded energy

Unable to be harnessed
Impossible to conceive
Celestially organic
Amongst us to believe

Phantom
_hydrus

I gave you
All my demons
You harnessed
Them with love
Slow was the deception
Their master you had become

One by one
My children
Burned at every stake
Turning to devour
Transformed to manipulate

My soul was yours in fire
Now casted spun in hate
Consumed I descended
Lost in a hypnotic state

Falsely you opressed me
Own these sins I earned
Slowly they digest you
The flames will make you burn

Alter
_hydrus

Torn and broken
Battered seed
Crumbled thorns
Scattered weeds

Left to die
In the desert air
Abandoned fossil
Rotting in despair

Within the rocks
There laid some shade
The night immersed
Paved a way

For this ground
Crept in the rain
It collected
To cease all pain

Now in stone
There is a friend
A new beginning
Forged to stand

And in this light
Leaves will thrive
Retell the tale
How death survived

Bloom
_hydrus

Hidden in meaning
Hunting to slay
Taking for giving
False prophets obey

Words used as spells
Blind the divine
Mixing injustice
Hailing to signs

Weak will recover
Dance in the night
Only to suffer
Exploited delight

Those who chant loudly
Dressed in their skin
Are fiends in hiding
To gain from your sins

Profit
_hydrus

Alone I wonder
What would have been
A new start
To a different end

Sheltered silence
Kept far away
In the clouds
A distant place

Everlasting breath
As I fly
Not a thought
Never a cry

Soaring as one
With the wind
Into the sun
Out of my skin

Free
-Hydrus

I was laying in darkness
You presented me light
Evicted my nightmares
Exploited my plight

Suffering in shadows
My end was unclear
Becoming my hero
Good fortune felt near

Unknown at the time
Your plans were to draw
Embracing my mercy
Grasping to claw

Dressed as my savior
I offered my soul
Empowered resistance
Harnessed control

Days became fruitless
Direction was lost
Inviting the wicked
Gave me my cross

Salvation
_hydrus

A simple flower
Dining on light
Unaware of
Her beautiful sight

Tainted waters
Fell in her well
Drained of sunshine
Untruthful spell

Curious locust
Join in the feast
Unhindered focus
Naive to eat

Rotted morsils
Consumed unpure
Wounded perfection
Absent the cure

Tainted
-Hydrus

Foolish to think that you were the cure
Senselessly risking to taste one unpure
Unwise the guessing of what someone sips
Thoughtless in nature and poison to lips

Impulsive
_hydrus

Caged behind
Bars of words
Ravaged wings
Sliced with swords

Chains bound
Rope may tie
Padded walls
Evil eyes

Watched and kept
Lock and key
Unaware of
such cruelty

Unbeknownst
Actions fade
Times misfortune
Acts in vain

Strength of will
Escaped release
One can't kill
A sacred peace

Holy
-Hydrus

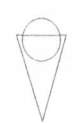

Disregard
The rules of life
Blindly entice
Carefree advice

Hang on virtues
Dangle in air
Fearless, idiotic
Selfishly unclear

Time will exploit
Turn black into gray
Morality's equal
Mauled in dismay

All that was thought
Now can be found
Aimlessly searching
In a world upside down

Oblivious
_hydrus

Taken
Forgotten
Expelled
Made rotten
Blamed
To be shamed
A toy
All a game
Felt
Now Feel
I am trash
My new real
All trust
Now gone
My fault
Born wrong

Fractured
-Hydrus

Careless monster
Quick to tempt
Indifferent manner
You spit contempt

Persuade and mimic
Unwise to scheme
Foolishly thoughtless
Knowingly mean

Abandoned actions
Misdeeds will call
Daring disaster
Plunging you fall

Misstep
_hydrus

I evolve
To dissolve

Build up
Just to crumble

Move ahead
As I retreat

Became a winner
In defeat

Found life
Just to lose

Start again
I must refuse

End
-Hydrus

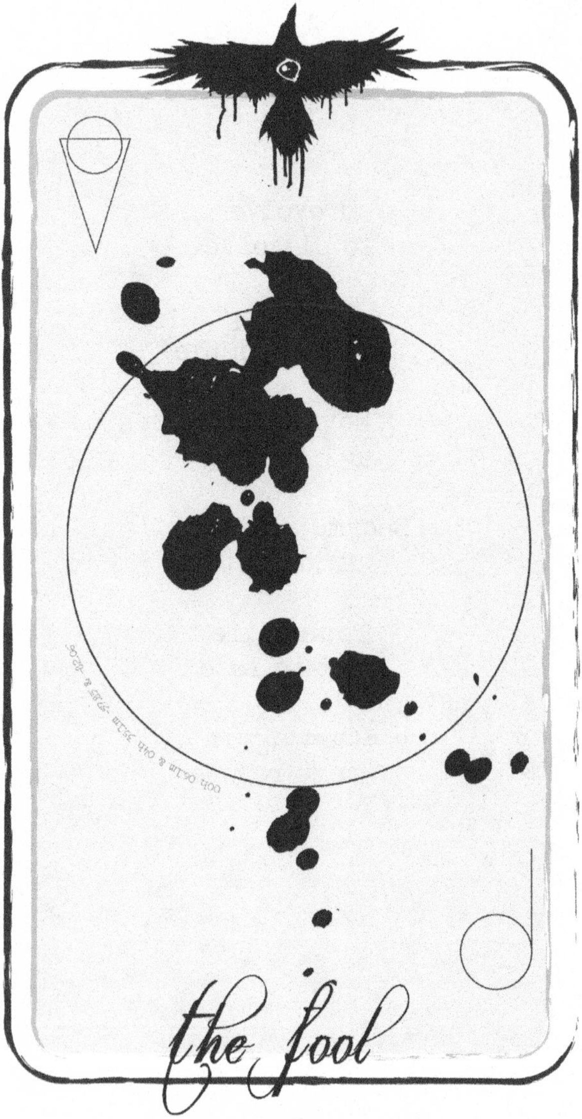
the fool

Reversed: recklessness, taken advantage of, inconsideration

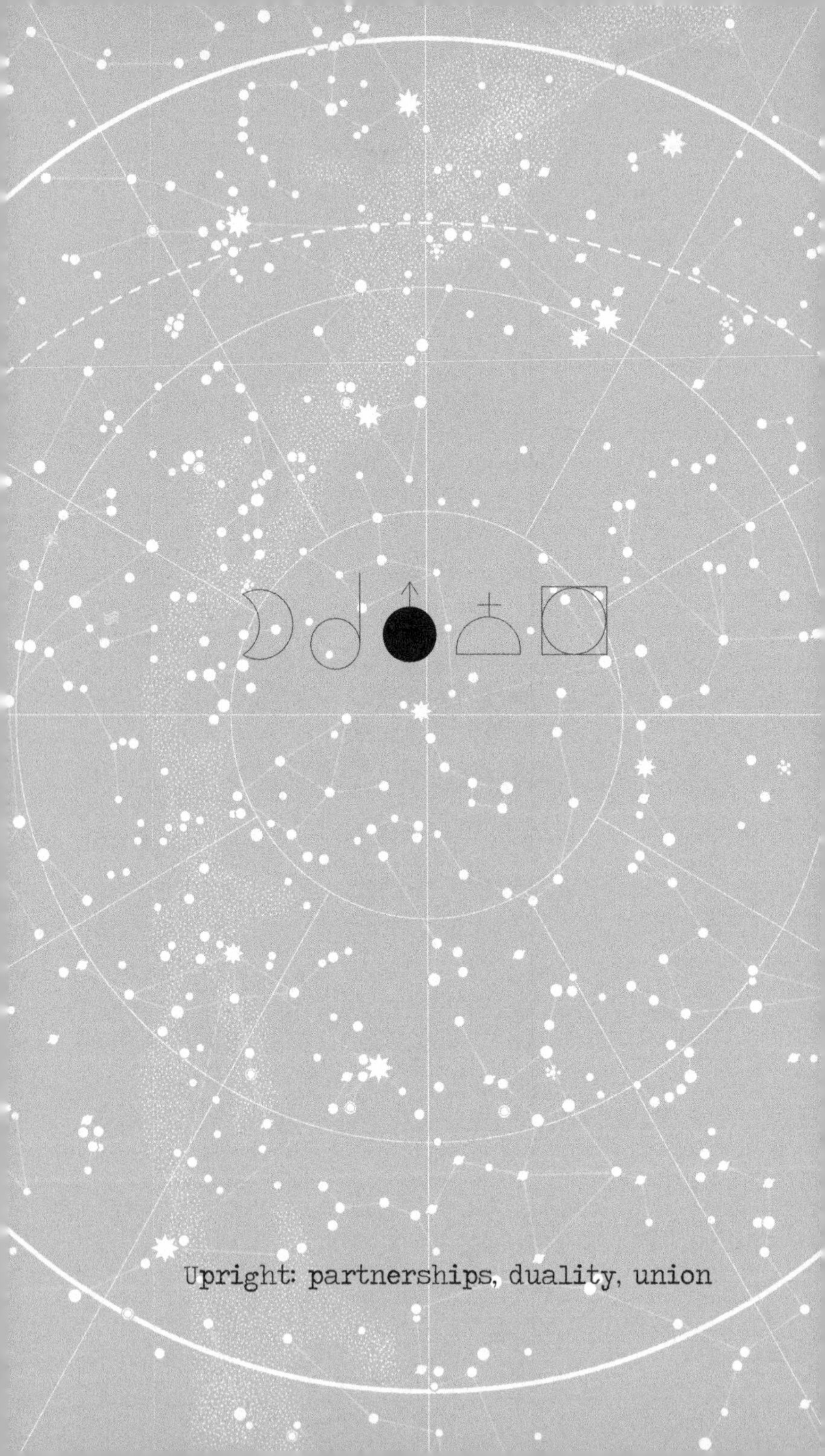

Upright: partnerships, duality, union

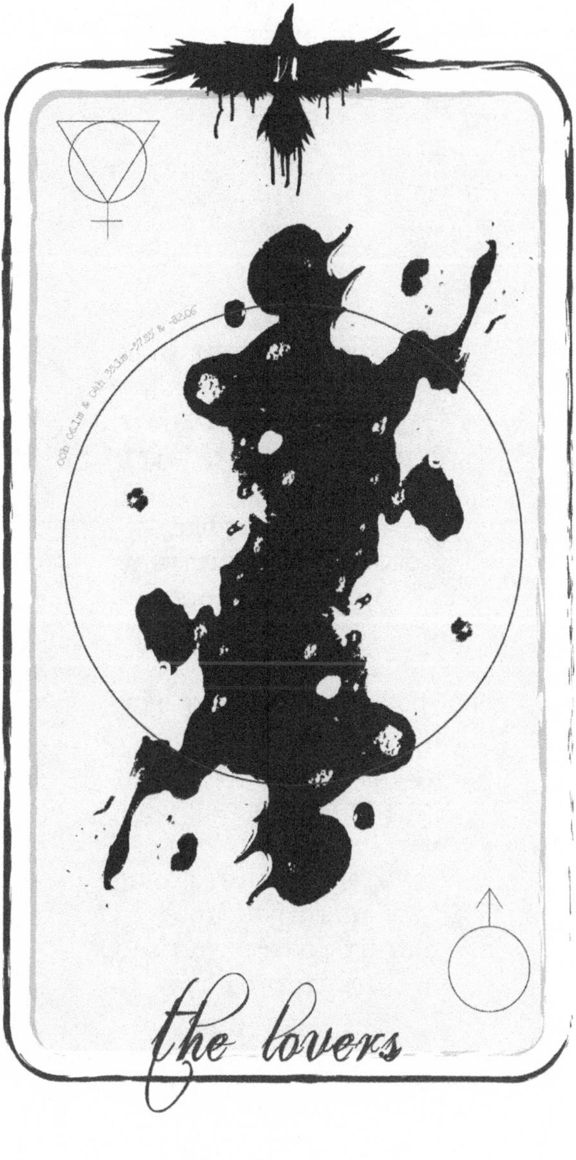
00h 04.1m & 04h 35.1m -57.55 & -82.06
the lovers

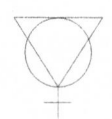

Left to dwindle
Roots splintered in heat
Scorched oasis
Dust blankets defeat

Once there were rains
Drenched and bathed
Washed over pain
Left lands unscathed

Now we wait
Shadows confide
Awaiting the swarms
Simply to hide

Life will be broken
A cycle complete
Harvested ghosts
Our maker we meet

Famine
_hydrus

♂

Running to you
A pace I will keep
Grasping to reach
Hands meant to meet

Destined in time
Stars vigorously preach
Perfectly sculpted
United to be

Shining in me
Unworthy retrieve
Humbled in nature
Tempted to leave

Connected in truth
One could not escape
Angelically written
Divine in her shape

Blessed presence
Emboldened as man
She is my savior
Cosmically planned

Written
_hydrus

You were my rock
My everlasting bond
A lighted pathway
Powerfully strong

Battles brought weakness
Humanity showed fear
An unstoppable being
The forces did not care

Unrelentless the struggle
Might fought with all will
Outnumbered by illness
Soon it would kill

I died on that day
Yet walk in the dark
My pillar was taken
Forever my spark

Unfair
_hydrus

Our fingers interlaced
In a vacuum of fate
Forever intertwined
A love claimed in faith

In your eyes I could dream
Of valleys and streams
Angelic choirs that sing
Upon placing my ring

Together
-hydrus

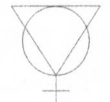

Helpless I grieve
A Lost companion
My world betrayed
Life deceived

Living in breath
Yearning to leave
Unable to function
Your soul unretrieved

Finding darkness
Unconscious my choice
United in guilt
We will rejoice

Promise
_hydrus

Inspired beauty
Breathless in your wake
Lost in your vision
A burning that I taste

Craving to devour
Trace every inch of skin
Longing for together
Our forever now begins

Us
-hydrus

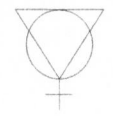

Without you I am hopeless
An unimagined sketch
A canvas unstretched
Graphite unetched

Emotionless dancers
Draped in nude
Quiet the still life
Unlit to seclude

Unframed portrait
A sky without clouds
An abandoned gesture
Unstippled in crowds

A linear moment
Defined to evoke
Brushed with your love
Eternal the stroke

Unfinished
_hydrus

♂

Captured
Trapped
Ensnared
By your grace
Entangled
In your presence
Bewitched by your stare
There are so many words
That can describe the spell
You have on me
It is eternal
Infinite
Only the gods
Can perceive my madness
For you

Fallen
_hydrus

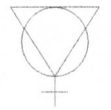

An angel is broken
Her wings are torn
I can fly
Make her reborn

Heal and soothe
Mend all wounds
Rebuild as whole
Upward soon

She also flew
A graceful flight
Reached the heavens
Left my sight

Unworthy
_hydrus

Seized by a whisper
A nibble at my ear
Fainted the touch
An embrace ever so near

Scent of an ocean
Waves in a breeze
Allowing to be open
Unhindered at ease

Wilted was the flower
Endangered to grow
Seeking all comfort
Lost in her glow

Held in my arms
Fleeing from the sea
Joined in the moment
Recovered to just be

Never abandoned
Always will protect
Completed my purpose
Will she forget

Habit
_hydrus

Why must you hold on
Feelings are ripped
Hearts insulted
Moments are sipped

Bodies are starved
Torn in existence
Built on circumstance
A vanished persistence

Convenient the dance
Armor covers our skin
Anger wields a shield
Approaching the end

Memories we steal
Erasing the past
Emotions unconcealed
This love will not last

Destined
_hydrus

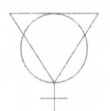

Tragic in my failure
To be a righteous soul
Doomed to be forgiven
Forsaken what I stole

Taken was a life
Unpure identity
Corrupted by my faults
Endangered in the greed

Unholy blinded merger
Selfish was the act
Love confused the moment
Altered in its pact

Attracted to the rage
Laced in what was had
Molded in a cage
Tormented to be mad

Unity confides
In what the devil brings
Gestured claws engaged
Bedded from within

Arraigned
_hydrus

I have never the answer
Corrected even in name
A quieted voice
Nothing to exclaim

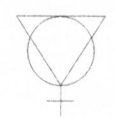

Opinions only carry
If listened in a jar
Silent the wanderer
A lost memory from far

Ignored
_hydrus

Wishful kisses
Graze my cheek
Subtle lips
Dipped to meet

Only to define
My stance
Engaged in wild
Dark romance

Only then will
Veils let you see
Unattained
Simplicities

What is had
Now is tossed
Stolen acts
All is lost

Greed
_hydrus

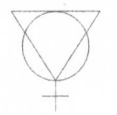

Why must I cry
Love only to die
Live for just living
Exist to always lie

Know
_hydrus

Black is the moment
All is real
White is the instance
One starts to conceal
All is imagined
Easy to detect
Inked are our flaws
Life will infect

Judged
_hydrus

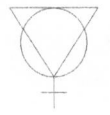

I am in pieces
Impossible to recover
All that was lost
The snows have now covered

At what cost
Faith has been challenged
Fractured in place
Hopelessly tangled

No one is willing
To fix my broken
Solve the empty
Undo the unspoken

Answers unanswered
Can someone save me
Humbly damaged
Begging I pray

Hope
_hydrus

♂

Darkness connects
As we infect our lust
Creative to dissect
Inclusive to indulge

Thirsting to digest
Juices flow to fill
Engorged in retrospect
Engulfed just to thrill

Perfect ceremony
Our moans escape to seek
Caught in defiance
Souls that truly feast

Together in our coffins
Twisted inhumane
Morbid our resilience
Tragic is our pain

Sentenced
_hydrus

Scorched roots
Buried in shame
A fraud to love
An actors game

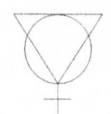

Foolish role
Willed by one
Reality twisted
Unmasked undone

Forever to bear
Life insincere
Souless in fear
Craven the tears

Coward
_hydrus

Living in a bubble
Glass has no walls
Forbidden and exhausted
Stricken to fall

Awakened from a slumber
Emotions unreal
Touched by an essence
A connection revealed

Far are the petals
That glisten in light
Removed are the doubts
Enabled to fight

A continued persistence
To feel what is real
Depicted in ink
An afflicted ordeal

Worlds are divided
In secret they grow
Embellished existence
Maternal the know

In absence they mourn
United they thrive
Unfair is this life
But their love will survive

Phoenix
_hydrus

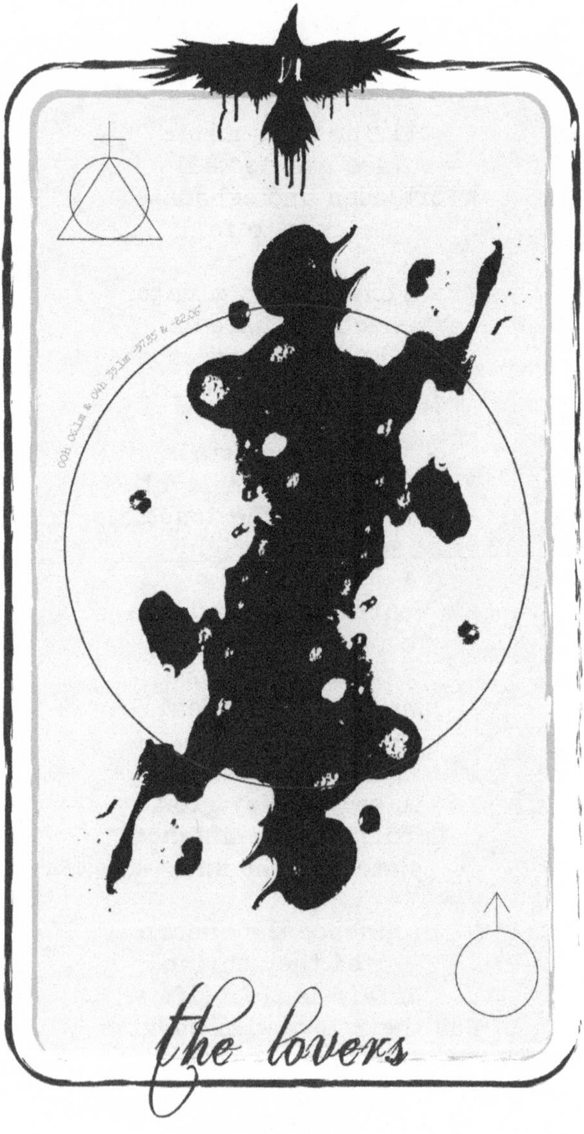
00h 06.1m & 04h 35.1m -57.85 & -82.06
the lovers

Reversed: loss of balance, one-sidedness, disharmony

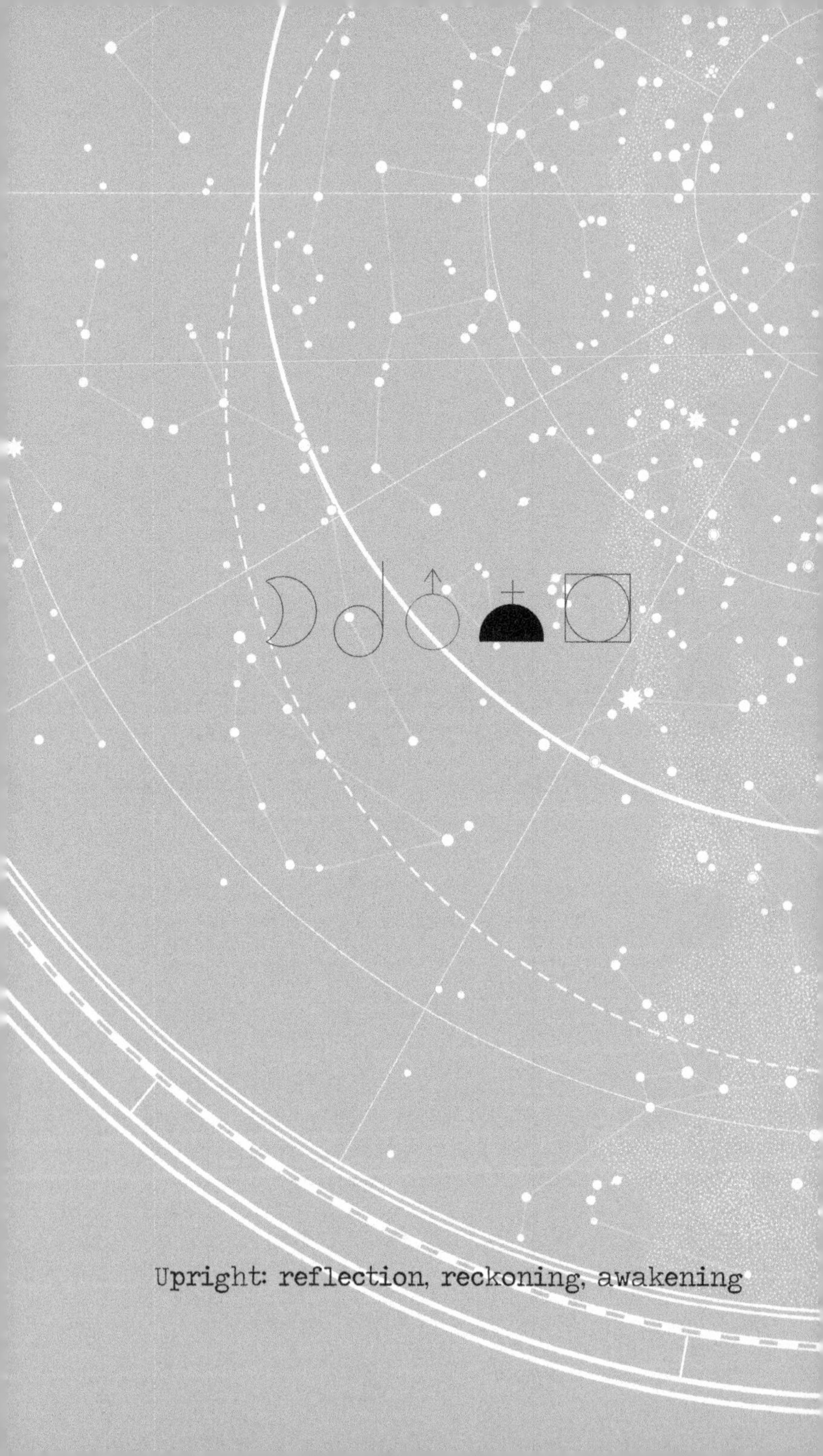

Upright: reflection, reckoning, awakening

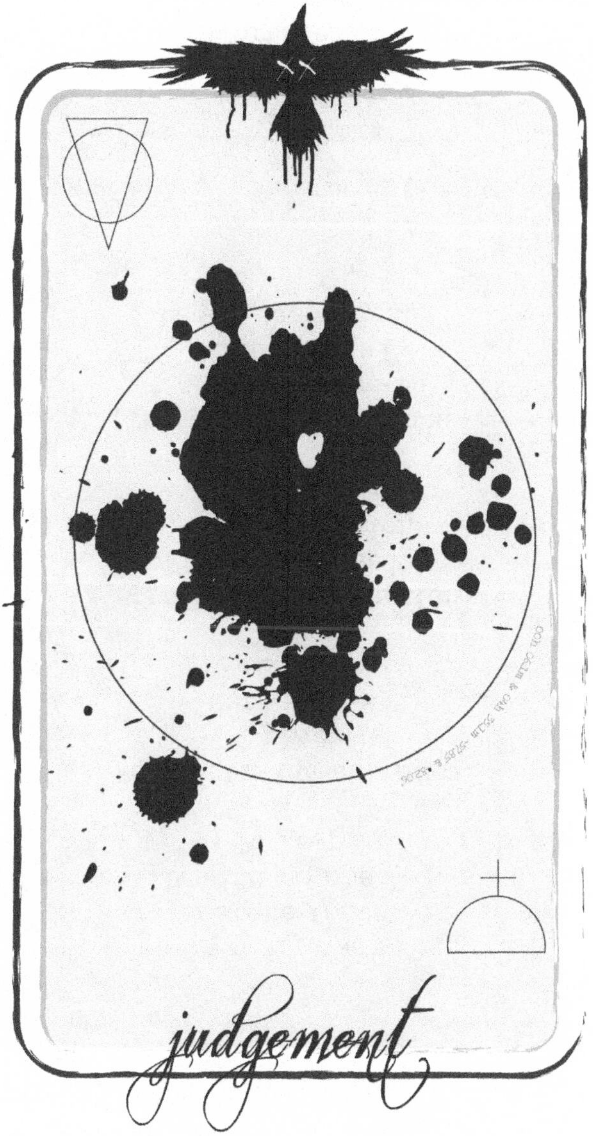
judgement

Wasting away
A stone fence
With no one
To keep

Forbidden the entrance
A place
Where home
Sleeps

Structured destruction
Planted in deeds
Awaiting erosion
Fallen the seed

The world is corroded
A shelter caved in
Buried denial
Demolished again

Worthless
_hydrus

A broken glimpse
Captures my past
Ripped observance
Of darkness cast

An Image torn
Insecure to hold
Deliberate gashes
Slashes of old

Painful reflections
Casting doubts
Thoughts betrayed
Emotions dry out

Never enough
Portrayed in flaws
Scratched illusions
Symptomatic fall

A stare inverted
Followed by tears
Engaged defiance
Mirrored in fear

Revealed
_hydrus

Morning has arrived
You quickly walk out
Troubled in silence
Cluttered in doubt

Having no direction
Embattled in despair
Losing you again
Emotions so unclear

What have I done
Crumbled in place
Exhausted all tears
Reliving your trace

Lessons not learned
Repeated to harm
Final this outcome
This was my charm

Trash
_hydrus

Waves in puddles
Tainted glass
An eyes reflection
A rippled past

Fictions weaver
Mending threads
Enabled scribbles
All mislead

Subtle rhythms
Define our craft
False afflictions
Unwritten drafts

Perceived perfection
Revealed ordeals
Lurk the monsters
Conceitedly real

Vanity
-hydrus

My soul
Will never be solved
It is cursed
With no one to love

An empty vessel
Marooned the ride
Vast is its fear
Isolated to hide

Everyone imagines
An escaped odyssey
Except my delusions
Trapped inside of me

Stranded
_hydrus

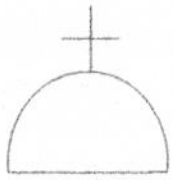

You never missed a chance
To let me feel your love
It was not a quick romance
But I gift from far above
You always held my hand
And never left my side
Until the moment came
When I lost you from my life

You
-hydrus

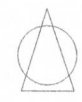

Follow me
If you want to fail
Never to win
Endless the sail

For this broken compass
Can never reach port
Lost in a voyage
Will always fall short

Suspicious the ocean
Scars that I bear
The life of the loser
An honor I wear

Cursed
_hydrus

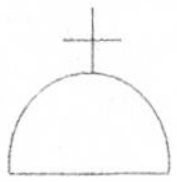

The day will come
When we will meet
Tears will fall
Words will flee
We will fight
All will lose
You will see
I will be true

Will
-hydrus

Will the sun attempt
To peak and glare its light
Show the world its path
Give life eternal sight

Or will it simply burn
Disappear as we seek
To fulfill our last devotions
Our dreams to just be free

Searching
_hydrus

You will pay
For the battered heart
You created
The doubt you buried
In my veins
A continuous
Poisoned stream
Of blackened angels
That ate
At my thoughts
Devouring my courage
To become me
A being
Consumed of light
Now just
A tainted match
In a puddle
Of confusion
Drowning
Misshapen
For the world
To crush
A flame
That will never
Live
Just be
Extinguished
From birth

Burnt
_hydrus

Alone in a room
Holding every key
No locks on the doors
Only misery

Not a corner to hide
Only shadowed in doubt
Unable to distinguish
My light has burned out

Closed
_hydrus

Silently you watch as I fail
My errors of life you travail
In solace you reap the rewards
Distant the juror explores

Never too far from my shame
Misguided the journey to blame
Allowing the stars to light fear
My horrors are tragically clear

Fate
_hydrus

Can I be the one
Who can pick up the pieces
Save you from you
Save you from me

No
_hydrus

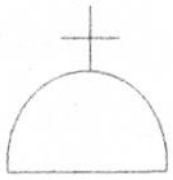

Your maker awaits
Tallies at hand
Of all misdeeds
Vile your plans

He will judge
A wrath be placed
Relived neglect
Ravaged disgrace

Banished your exit
Ceased from Life
A toll now paid
Eternal the strife

Endured to suffer
Failed in kind
Mistaken for Human
Flames will remind

Condemned
_hydrus

Tired of the struggle
A constant battle to win
Unable to function
Uninformed to comprehend

I cannot breathe
Rendered is my story
Afflicted by the demons
Humiliated in glory

My flag flies torn
Waving without a home
Scorched in its place
My walls have fallen down

Overtaken
_hydrus

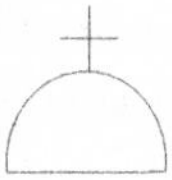

The night brought me you
An endless sky of painted stars
Everlasting love that seemed limitless
A horizon less dusk of emotions
Until the sun awoke and you were gone

Predictable
_hydrus

Vile ashes
Rain to prey
Wicked tongues
Casted away

Loathsomely blackened
Where dust breathes wind
Contempt in emotions
Bastardly kin

Birthed to be blind
Forgettably crude
Vain in reflection
Offensively lude

Dreams will await
Demands to be made
Prayers for justice
Life will soon fade

Denied
_hydrus

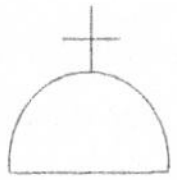

It took a thousand broken hearts
To make me forget you
It will take a thousand more
For me to love again

Shamed
_hydrus

Unaware of the hurt
Running away from the pain
A constant reminder
Of nothing ever gained

Unexploited worth
A single piano key
Untouched forgiveness
Wasted melody

Silently forgotten
An unforgiving tune
Always the burden
Pathetically immune

Tainted
_hydrus

Life remembered
That one existed
Damned
To a soulless earth
An empty carcass
Of a man
That never slept
Just searched
To be taken back
Boundless
In a darkness
Where his soul
Starvingly wept

Homeless
_hydrus

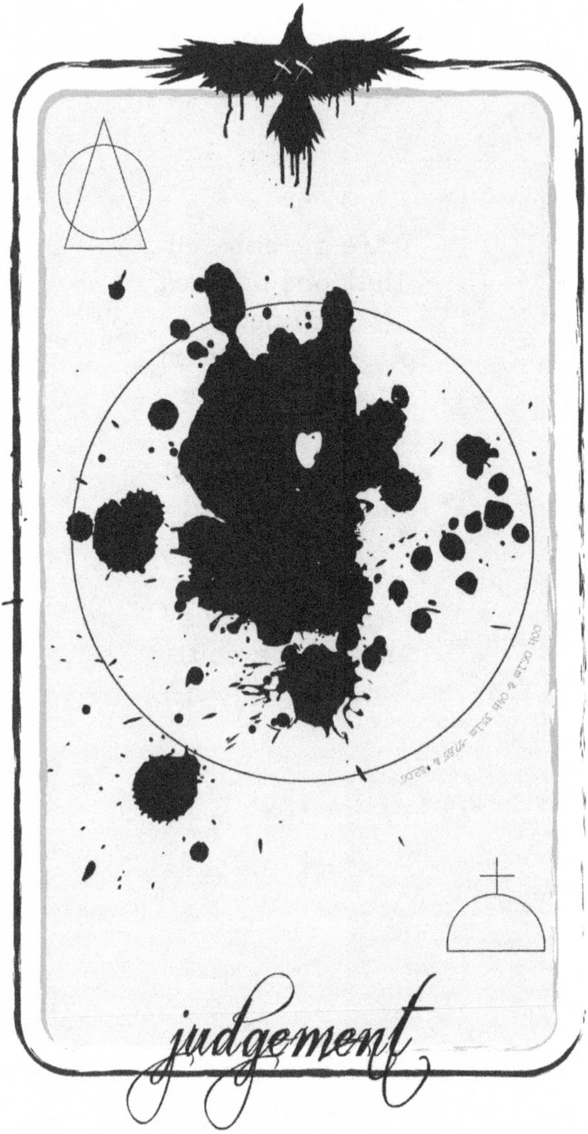
judgement

Reversed: lack of self awareness, doubt,
self loathing

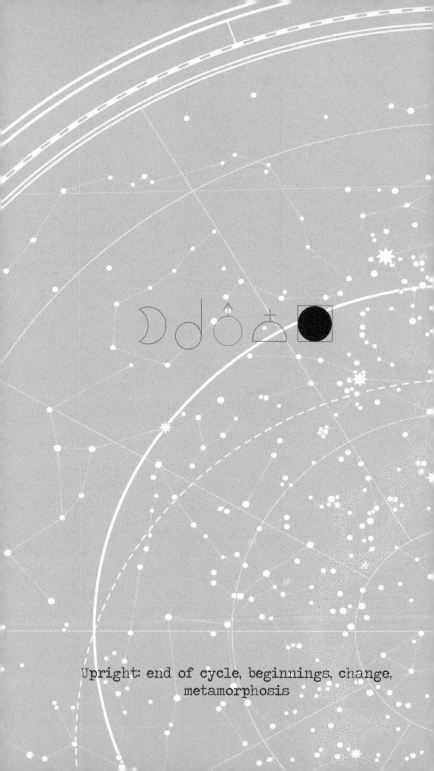

Upright: end of cycle, beginnings, change, metamorphosis

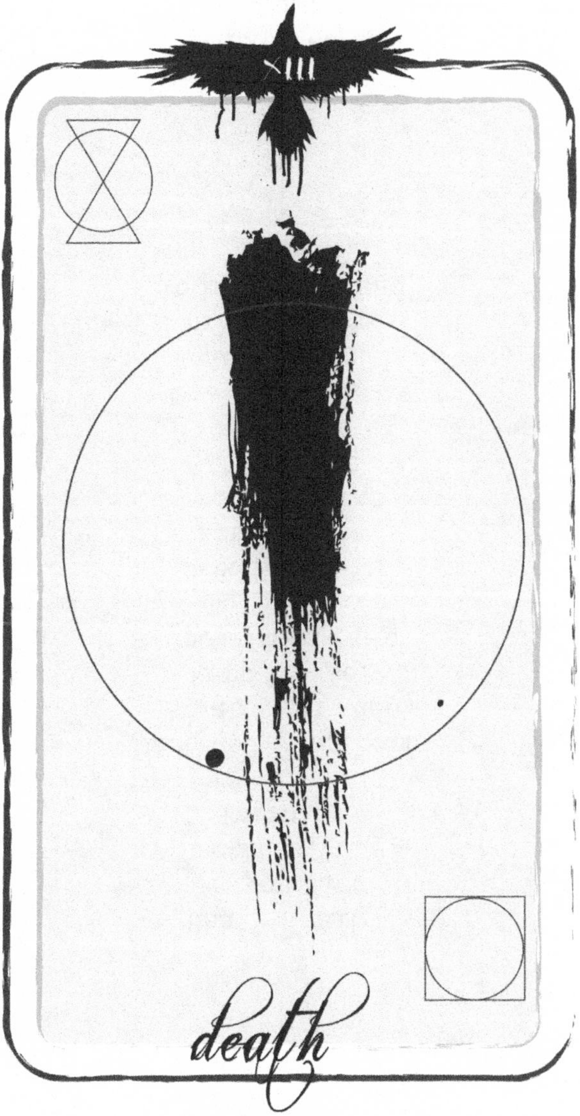
XIII
death

Death awaits
As you flee
Destined home
Infinity

Plagued when born
A watchers keep
Kept in view
For him to reap

Deeds in skin
Actions met
Prompted sins
All preset

One has breath
Exists as dead
Fall has come
To meet your end

Expired
_hydrus

Beyond the storms
The ravens fly
Hunting souls
Thirsting demise

A scavenged flight
Pursued to ingest
Clawing at vengeance
Tasting regrets

Devouring you whole
Deleting intent
Extracting your soul
Exclaiming repent

Voraciously chewed
Wings painted red
Prayers refused
Sins of the dead

Ousted
_hydrus

A crumbled stone
With no name
Adorns the site
Crimes reclaimed

Simple rock
Marked in place
Symbolizing
Your wicked trace

Here you lay
A stifled form
Muzzled dry
Decomposed

Heated ground
Spirits speak
Feasting flames
Underneath

Roast
_hydrus

End is upon us
The winged angels cry
Trumpets and chariots
Fill a bloodied sky

Demons have vanquished
Served masters their fate
Allegiance to darkness
Banished from gates

Heavens run empty
Masses hail faith
Time disregarded
Forgiveness too late

Eternity
_hydrus

At my feet you beg and scream
Gnawing at a distant dream
Buried in the mud you choke
Taking back the hate you spoke

Ravens watch as you lapse
Idly savoring muted gasps
Rotten earth becomes your bed
Decayed descent engulfs your head

Riddance
_hydrus

Received the news
Your space awaits
Deep the trench
A solemn space

In this cavern
You will sleep
Watch the earth
All that creeps

Such a perfect
Place to be
Surrounded with
Your destiny

May this slumber
Only ease
Lives you left
Now at peace

Remains
_hydrus

Inside I rot
Dismal and gray
Worms dig in
Twirl and play

Fruitless corpse
Dressed in vines
Ragged wears
Dust in time

Final peace
Caverned dwell
Banished from
A wasted cell

Gambled chances
Eroded paths
Collapsed romances
Squandered acts

As a host
I truly failed
A journey lost
One last exhale

Breakup
_hydrus

A deepened soul
Drenched in rain
Poured revival
A wilting strain

Rooted life
Succumb to change
Woven petals
Far reaching pain

Lifted seasons
As the dust dries
Transformations
Under dark skies

Seeded vines
Of a lunar spawn
Ascending demons
Throughout the dawn

Clouded cycles
Of a winding path
Morphing states
Unbrindled wrath

Resurgent
_hydrus

Devils laugh at my stake
In trusting you with my ache
The pain I hold you create
A fatal death to make

Widows claim to eat their mates
Serve them on hanging plates
Poison spun with so much ease
Regardless you chose to please

Captured on this web I live
Hosting all the ills you give
Longing to be your kill
Knowing I never will

Caught
_hydrus

Slowly your roses turned into weeds
Hideously seeking a love to impede
Perfumed with the poison to candidly spark
Hidden her secret infectiuosly dark

Wretched
_hydrus

A touch
A call
A note
A song
A memory
A smell
A word
My hell

Anything I can
To keep you close to me

When all I have
Is this exhausting agony

Knowing you are gone
I will never just be

I will carry you
Eternally

Together
_hydrus

At first it was
A love so blind
Enamored by
Angels of time

Destined to
Unite in bliss
One day sealed
By heavens kiss

Unknown to one
A fade began
Subtle haze
Took all command

No more wings
And halos faith
Misguided trust
In our state

Wings had turned
To fiery horns
Unfounded scorn
The bond was torn

An appetite
Grew in mistrust
Triggered by
Forbidden lusts

Creative gestures
Used to please
Souless creatures
Faked appease

All was lost
In a morbid sense
Life misplaced
No recompense

Tragic
_hydrus

Simple things that make us glow
Placed by kisses meant to show

Are the bonds that two create
Solidified an everlasting date

Humankind will try to break
Illuminate all of ones mistakes

In this time one must grow
Unite in love and not let go

Trial
_hydrus

Fatal is the ending
Where my soul
had crashed

Simple its conclusion
Tragically
it passed

Regardless of awareness
All it knew was gone

Ending without extinction
Life will go on

Cycle
_hydrus

Lost all I knew
When you left
Drowned in sadness
A sudden theft

Taken from me
My everything
The sun that rose
Colors of Spring

Breathe of air
A guiding light
The will to live
Ones drive to fight

Eternal anchor
Grounded the sky
Dimmed existence
My star has died

Gone
_hydrus

I commit to this journey
Engaged in the unknown
A voyage of discovery
One not taken alone

Bound by devotion
Embraced empathy
Pure the emotion
Enlightened destiny

_We begin
hydrus

You are my normal
Invested I am
Fulfilled as a person
Completed as man

In us I am grounded
My valleys are few
Our time intertwined
My feelings are true

All that I need
Is found in your heart
Seasons will change
We shall not depart

If the storms come
Dividing our will
Together we stand
For you I would kill

Forever
_hydrus

How could you wonder
About the sins of old
Rumors and stories
Actions turned cold

Bitter existence
Fled from the past
Into your arms
Felt peace at last

Judge me for now
The person you met
End preconceptions
Of what I had left

Inside me I hurt
Memories still stalk
Make a decision
To stay or to walk

Decide
-hydrus

An altered state
I cannot control
Horrified actions
Anxiety unfolds

A time for chance
Unknown the play
Evolving truths
Suggested ways

Amended versions
Revolving mistakes
Imposing revisions
Disrupted delays

Lost my direction
My sight was impaled
Excuses unfinished
True anguish unveiled

Duress
_hydrus

You came as an angel
All sainted in joy
Swept were your wings
Brilliant the ploy

Under your strands
Laying in wait
Dormant the horns
Staging my fate

Once vilified
Words would attack
Seeking to ambush
Forcing one back

Stunned evolution
A beauty so scorned
Destructively vain
Tormentingly torn

A halo now broken
Heavens mistake
Odd premonition
Unholy the mate

Epiphany
_hydrus

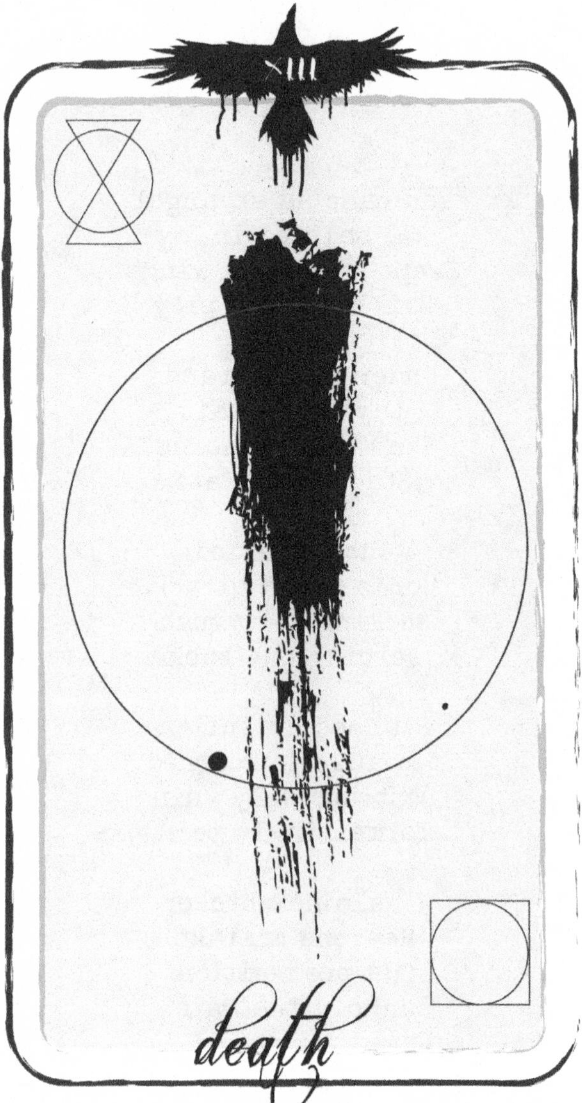
XIII
death

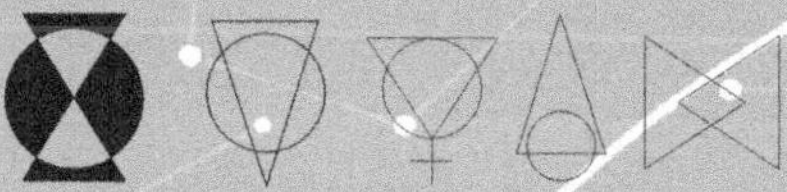

Reversed: fear of change, holding on,
stagnation, decay

∞

To all my loved ones who continue to shape my journey into the infinite shadows here and beyond

Thank You

C./G.

Thank You

"Never to suffer would never to have been blessed."

-Edgar Allan Poe

Also by _hydrus

ENDVISIBLE

A collection of poems about the endless feeling of being invisible while going through the emotions and sometimes cruelties of life. Illustrated by the author's own photography, this book guides us through grief, loss and love in a dark and inspiring way typical to how Hydrus's writing helps us cope with reality.

About The Author

Anonymous poet, photographer and artist, Hydrus documents through his poems the darkness and the glimmers of life taunting us when we are in the shadows, as well as many of the little things which make a colossal impact on who we are.

Connect with hydrus:

Website: www.hydruspoetry.com
Instagram: instagram.com/hydruspoetry
Facebook: https://www.facebook.com/hydruspoetry